REMARKABLE
PEOPLE

LeBron James

by Anita Yasuda

MEDIA ENHANCED BOOKS
AV²
BY WEIGL
ADDED VALUE • AUDIO VISUAL

www.av2books.com

AV² provides enriched content that supplements and complements this book. Weigl's AV² books strive to create inspired learning and engage young minds in a total learning experience.

Your AV² Media Enhanced books come alive with...

Audio
Listen to sections of the book read aloud.

Key Words
Study vocabulary, and complete a matching word activity.

Go to www.av2books.com, and enter this book's unique code.

BOOK CODE

J526956

Video
Watch informative video clips.

Quizzes
Test your knowledge.

Embedded Weblinks
Gain additional information for research.

Slide Show
View images and captions, and prepare a presentation.

AV² by Weigl brings you media enhanced books that support active learning.

Try This!
Complete activities and hands-on experiments.

... and much, much more!

Published by AV² by Weigl
350 5th Avenue, 59th Floor
New York, NY 10118

www.av2books.com   www.weigl.com

Library of Congress Cataloging-in-Publication Data

Yasuda, Anita.
  Lebron James / Anita Yasuda.
     p. cm. -- (Remarkable people)
  Includes index.
  ISBN 978-1-61690-669-6 (hardcover : alk. paper) -- ISBN 978-1-61690-674-0 (softcover : alk. paper)
  1. James, LeBron--Juvenile literature. 2. Basketball players--United States--Biography--Juvenile literature. I. Title.
  GV884.J36W43 2011
  796.323092--dc22
  [B]
                                    2010051003

Printed in the United States of America in North Mankato, Minnesota
1 2 3 4 5 6 7 8 9 0 15 14 13 12 11

WEP37500
052011

Editor: Heather Kissock
Design: Terry Paulhus

Photograph Credits
Weigl acknowledges Getty Images as the primary image supplier for this title.

Every reasonable effort has been made to trace ownership and to obtain permission to reprint copyright material. The publishers would be pleased to have any errors or omissions brought to their attention so that they may be corrected in subsequent printings.

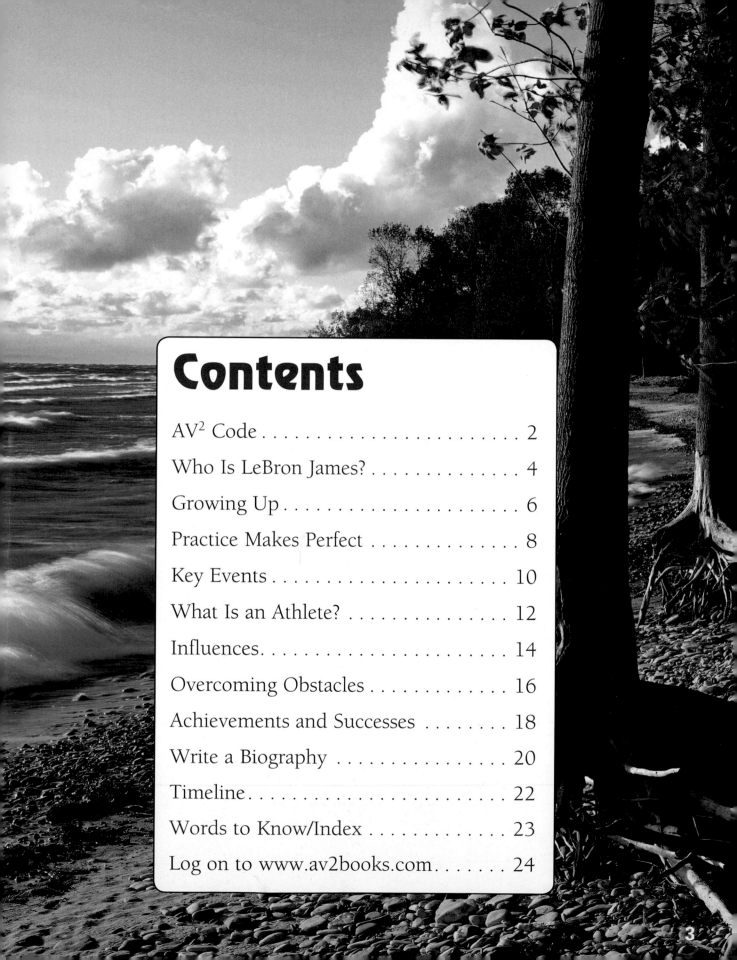

Contents

Who Is LeBron James?

LeBron James is one of the National Basketball Association's (NBA's) top players. Known for his speed and skill, he rarely allows other players to take the ball away or block his shots. His abilities have led sports magazines to give him nicknames such as The Chosen One and King James.

LeBron has dominated basketball courts since his teen years in Akron, Ohio. After turning **professional**, he played for the Cleveland Cavaliers for seven seasons. During this time, he earned two Most Valuable Player (MVP) awards. In 2010, he joined the Miami Heat.

"There is a lot of pressure put on me, but I don't put a lot of pressure on myself. I feel if I play my game, it will take care of itself."

LeBron is very active in his community. He developed the LeBron James Family Foundation to help single-parent families that are experiencing problems. The foundation provides programs that focus on building strong family units.

Growing Up

LeBron James was born on December 30, 1984, in Akron, Ohio. His mother Gloria was only 16 at the time. Gloria raised LeBron on her own. Gloria and LeBron moved many times during his childhood.

LeBron showed early athletic skill. When he was still a toddler, his mother gave him a ball and hoop set. LeBron played with his new toy for hours. This love for sports continued when LeBron began school, where he gained a reputation for being good at both basketball and football.

His home life made it difficult for LeBron to fit in with other students. He was constantly changing schools and having to make new friends. His grades suffered due to the lack of **stability**. Gloria knew there was a problem. When LeBron was in fifth grade, she agreed to let LeBron live with his football coach, Frank Walker, and his family.

■ LeBron and his mother have always had a close relationship.

Get to Know Ohio

Michigan · Ontario · Indiana · Kentucky · West Virginia

0 — 50 Miles
0 — 50 Kilometers

FLOWER
Scarlet Carnation

TREE
Ohio Buckeye

BIRD
Cardinal

The birthplace of Ulysses S. Grant, military leader and 18th president of the United States, is in Point Pleasant, Ohio. The site is now a designated National Historic Landmark.

Columbus is the capital of Ohio.

Campbell Hill is the highest point in Ohio. It is 1,550 feet (472 meters) high.

Neil Armstrong, the first man to set foot on the Moon, was born in Wapakoneta, Ohio, in 1930.

Think about it!

Athletes are often asked to **endorse** products. They have their names on shoes, and specific styles are created just for them. The products are then sold in stores all over the country. If you were a star athlete and were being paid to endorse a product to your fans, what would you do with the money you earned from endorsements? Would you donate any to **charity**?

Practice Makes Perfect

By the time LeBron entered high school, he was known as an excellent athlete, especially in basketball. At St. Vincent-St. Mary High School, in Akron, he became a member of the Fighting Irish, the school's basketball team. With his help, the team won every game that season and also won the state championship. The Fighting Irish then went on to win the national championship as well.

LeBron's skill on the basketball court brought him much attention. The attention increased when he began breaking records. By the end of his high-school basketball career, LeBron had scored more than 2,600 points, 500 assists, and almost 900 **rebounds**. This display of talent won LeBron Ohio's "Mr. Basketball" title three times. This title is given out each year to the top high school basketball player in the state.

■ LeBron was the youngest player in Ohio to ever be given the Mr. Basketball title.

By 2002, LeBron was gaining national attention. Players from other teams would ask for his autograph. College coaches, NBA **scouts,** and NBA superstar Shaquille O'Neal came to watch him play. Athletic shoe companies wanted to sign him to an advertising **contract**. LeBron had not even turned professional yet. He was still a high school student.

During LeBron's last year of school, rumors surfaced that he would go straight to the NBA. These rumors were true. At the age of 19, LeBron became the first pick in the 2003 NBA **draft**. He was drafted by the Cleveland Cavaliers. LeBron's first year as an NBA player was outstanding. He won **Rookie** of the Year for the 2003–2004 season. LeBron was the first Cavalier and the youngest player ever to win that honor.

■ The Cavaliers had been near the bottom of the NBA rankings before LeBron joined the team. By the end of his first year, they were playoff contenders.

LeBron was attracting attention for his basketball skills while still in high school. On a cover of Sports Illustrated, he was called "The Chosen One." ESPN began to broadcast his high school games nationally. Other countries also began to notice his skills as a basketball player.

When LeBron began playing for the Cleveland Cavaliers, he had to prove that he was more than a high school star. LeBron did not disappoint. In his rookie year, LeBron averaged nearly 21 points per game. He also became the youngest player to score more than 40 points in a single game.

His successes as a Cavalier continued. He led the team to the 2005–2006 playoffs for the first time in seven seasons. The next year, he took the Cavaliers to the finals. However, in 2010, LeBron decided he needed a change. He left the Cleveland Cavaliers to joint the Miami Heat.

■ Lebron James and his teammates on the U.S. men's basketball team won the gold medal at the 2008 Olympics in Beijing, China.

Thoughts from LeBron

James has always loved basketball. Here are some of the things he has said about playing professionally.

James appreciates being a basketball player.
"Glamor and all that stuff don't excite me. I am just glad I have the game of basketball in my life."

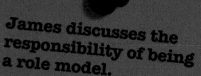

James discusses the responsibility of being a role model.
"As athletes, we work hard for what we get. But at the same time, we should work even harder to lay down the stones so that it's much easier for the youth coming up."

James strives to be a team player.
"To all the positions, I just bring the determination to win. Me being an unselfish player, I think that can carry on to my teammates."

James talks about his greatest fear.
"My greatest fear is probably myself. Can I continue to push myself to bigger heights? With everyone counting on me, it is all about, 'Can I push myself to be better?'"

James shares his family's reaction to his move to Miami.
"They're happy to see me happy. That's what they can see in my face. They say: 'It's been a while since we've seen you look like that'."

James is grateful for the lessons he learned when he was young.
"I know my background, know what my mother went through. I never get too high on my stardom or what I can do."

What Is an Athlete?

A thletes are people who play sports or participate in other highly physical activities. Professional athletes are people who make their living doing this. Amateur athletes are those who play sports in their spare time.

Professional athletes must stay in good physical condition at all times. They train and practice constantly to stay fit and maintain their skills. Often, certain exercises are required. The type of exercises depends on the sport the athlete plays. Even in the off-season, athletes must keep up their physical fitness through diet and exercise.

Athletic people often use their skills to further their education. Many schools offer sports **scholarships** to good amateur athletes. These scholarships pay for an athlete's **tuition**.

■ Some athletes go on to teach or coach. In this way, they pass on their knowledge to the next generation. Former Cavaliers coach Paul Silas once played with the Boston Celtics.

Athletes 101

Shaun White (1986–)

Shaun White is a professional snowboarder and skateboarder. He has won many awards in both sports and is considered one of the greatest **extreme athletes** in the world. Shaun first began snowboarding when he was six years old. By 13 years of age, he was snowboarding professionally. When he was 17, he became a professional skateboarder as well. In 2003, Shaun became the first athlete to win medals in both the Winter and Summer X Games. Shaun also participated in two Winter Olympics. He won one gold medal at each event.

Samuel Bode Miller (1977–)

Samuel Bode Miller is an alpine ski racer. He has been the world champion in this event four times. At World Cup races, he competes in all five events: slalom, giant slalom, Super G, downhill, and combined. He has won in all five events. Bode has won 32 World Cup events. At the 2010 Vancouver Winter Olympics, he won Olympic medals in the Super G, super combined, and downhill.

Misty May-Treanor (1977–)

With 107 wins, Misty May-Treanor has won more volleyball tournaments than any other female volleyball player in history. Misty played in her first beach-volleyball tournament when she was eight. She continued to play throughout her youth and into university. Over the course of her career, she has received many honors and awards, including a gold medal at both the 2004 and 2008 Summer Olympics.

Apolo Ohno (1982–)

Apolo Ohno is an Olympic speed skating champion. He was born in Seattle, Washington. Apolo became interested in short-track speed skating when he was 12 years old. Two years later, he became the youngest skater admitted to the Lake Placid Olympic Training Center. In 1997, Apolo became the youngest U.S. National Speed Skating Champion. He has won more medals than any other Winter Olympic athlete from the United States. He has two gold, two silver, and four bronze medals.

The Olympics

The Olympic Games began almost 3,000 years ago in the town of Olympia in Ancient Greece. The Olympics were held every four years in August or September and were a showcase of athletic talent. The games continued until about 400 AD, when they were stopped by the Roman emperor. They were not held again for more than 1,500 years. In 1896, the first modern Olympics took place in Athens, Greece. In 1924, the first Winter Olympics were held in Chamonix, France.

Influences

Leron's life changed when his mother let him go to live with the Walker family. The Walker family provided a stable environment for LeBron. He was treated like one of the family. Like the other Walker children, he had to do chores and help around the house. LeBron also started attending school regularly. He even earned his school's attendance award in grade 5.

Growing up, LeBron admired Michael Jordan. He liked the way Michael approached the game, his commitment to it, and his leadership skills. Michael, like LeBron, excelled in basketball. He won five regular season MVP awards, six NBA championships, six NBA Finals MVP awards, three **All-Star Game** MVP awards, and a Defensive Player of the Year award.

■ Michael Jordan wore the number 23 on his team jersey for most of his career.

LeBron chose the number 23 in honor of his idol. He later changed to number 6 out of respect for Michael Jordan. When LeBron was in his third year at high school, he was invited to a gym in Chicago for a workout with Michael and other NBA players. Here, Michael told LeBron to keep working hard, and someday he would get to the NBA. LeBron followed his advice and became an NBA player.

THE LEBRON JAMES FAMILY

LeBron's mother, Gloria, is one of LeBron's biggest fans. Gloria is usually seated courtside at all of his home games. Gloria even gets into arguments with players on opposing teams when she feels that they have intentionally **fouled** her son. LeBron's girlfriend, Savannah Brinson, and their two children, LeBron James Jr. and Bryce Maximus, are also big fans.

■ LeBron's mother, girlfriend, and children often attend his games.

Overcoming Obstacles

LeBron faced many obstacles growing up. He was raised in poverty. The areas of Akron where his mother could afford to live were filled with violence. His mother protected him from the violence as much as possible. Still, he experienced situations that many children do not. When he went to live with his football coach, he had more stability in his life.

In high school, LeBron led St. Vincent-St. Mary to three state championships. Sports reporters described his play as spectacular. He was in constant demand for interviews and public appearances. At times, LeBron's celebrity became overwhelming. It was challenging for him to concentrate on basketball. LeBron relied on his friends and family to keep him grounded.

■ LeBron is constantly in demand for interviews before and after games.

It takes hard work and determination to make it into the NBA. It takes even more work to be a star player. LeBron found his rookie year tough in the NBA. He was starting his career and had to prove himself in the world of professional basketball. He felt that he was just a beginner. LeBron had confidence in his abilities. He knew that he would do his best for his team. LeBron has said that the experiences he had during his rookie year made him a better player.

■ Even though LeBron had difficulties adjusting to life as an NBA player, he remained focused on being a good basketball player. This focus was rewarded when he won the Rookie of the Year award.

Achievements and Successes

LeBron has had much success in his basketball career. In the 2004–2005 season, LeBron started in 80 games. He was named to the All-NBA Team. This is an honor given to the best players in the NBA at the end of every season. LeBron was the youngest player in league history to be given All-NBA honors.

LeBron continued to break NBA records. In 2005, he averaged an amazing 30 points a game. He was the youngest player in NBA history to play at this level. Due to LeBron's determination, Cleveland finished second in the Central Division. This was the first time the Cavaliers reached the playoffs in eight years. On March 20, 2005, LeBron became the youngest player to score at least 50 points in a game. He scored 56 points against the Toronto Raptors.

■ LeBron was named to the NBA All-Star team in 2010. The All-Stars were divided into two teams, representing east and west. LeBron played on the East team at the All-Star game in Arlington, Texas.

During the 2007–2008 season, LeBron became the youngest player ever to hit the 10,000-point mark. He also became the **franchise**'s all-time leading scorer. In his final year with the Cleveland Cavaliers, the team finished with 61 wins out of 82 games, the NBA's top victory total. LeBron averaged 29.7 points a game. It was no surprise that he won the MVP award that year.

HELPING OTHERS

In 2004, LeBron established the LeBron James Family Foundation. Its goal is to help children be physically fit and do well at school. LeBron hosts an annual King for Kids Bikeathon in Akron. The event helps local families.

In 2008, the LeBron James Family Foundation launched a national program to build safe playgrounds across the United States. The foundation sponsors a variety of events and activities to help families.

Write a Biography

A person's life story can be the subject of a book. This kind of book is called a biography. Biographies describe the lives of remarkable people, such as those who have achieved great success or have done important things to help others. These people may be alive today, or they may have lived many years ago. Reading a biography can help you learn more about a remarkable person.

At school, you might be asked to write a biography. First, decide who you want to write about. You can choose a athlete, such as LeBron James, or any other person. Then, find out if your library has any books about this person. Learn as much as you can about him or her. Write down the key events in this person's life. What was this person's childhood like? What has he or she accomplished? What are his or her goals? What makes this person special or unusual?

A concept web is a useful research tool. Read the questions in the following concept web. Answer the questions in your notebook. Your answers will help you write your biography.

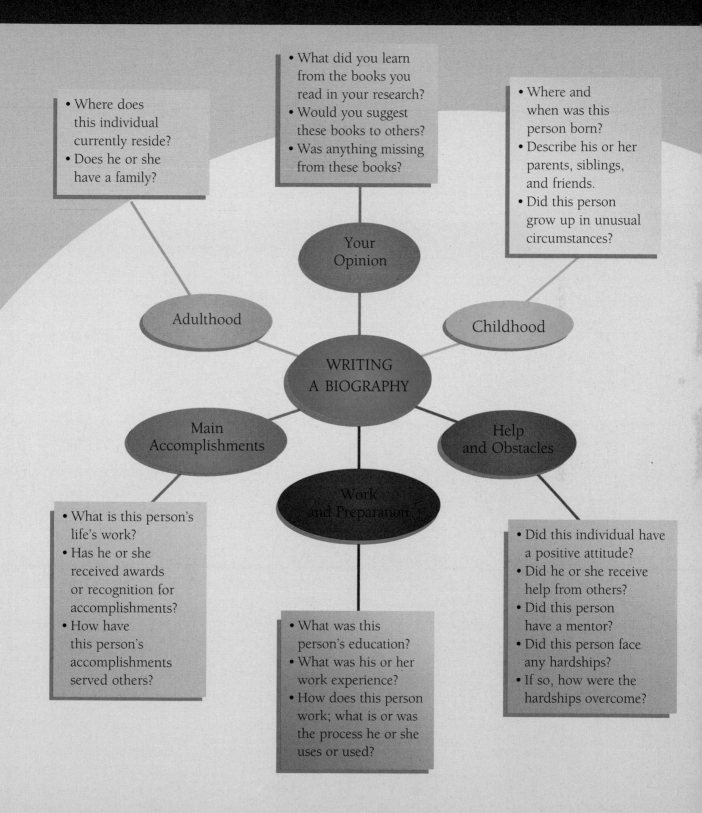

- Where does this individual currently reside?
- Does he or she have a family?

- What did you learn from the books you read in your research?
- Would you suggest these books to others?
- Was anything missing from these books?

- Where and when was this person born?
- Describe his or her parents, siblings, and friends.
- Did this person grow up in unusual circumstances?

Your Opinion

Adulthood

Childhood

WRITING A BIOGRAPHY

Main Accomplishments

Help and Obstacles

Work and Preparation

- What is this person's life's work?
- Has he or she received awards or recognition for accomplishments?
- How have this person's accomplishments served others?

- Did this individual have a positive attitude?
- Did he or she receive help from others?
- Did this person have a mentor?
- Did this person face any hardships?
- If so, how were the hardships overcome?

- What was this person's education?
- What was his or her work experience?
- How does this person work; what is or was the process he or she uses or used?

Timeline

YEAR	LEBRON JAMES	WORLD EVENTS
1984	LeBron James is born on December 30 in Akron, Ohio.	The United States Olympic Men's Basketball team wins the gold medal at the Olympic Games in Los Angeles.
1995	LeBron joins The Shooting Stars, an amateur basketball team.	The Chicago Bulls win their fourth NBA Championship.
1999	LeBron begins playing for St. Vincent-St. Mary High School basketball team the Fighting Irish.	Cyclist Lance Armstrong wins the Tour de France.
2001	LeBron is awarded Ohio's Mr. Basketball title for the first time.	Shaquille O'Neal is the NBA Finals MVP.
2003	LeBron is the number one pick in the NBA draft by the Cleveland Cavaliers.	Sammy Sosa hits his 500th career home run.
2008	LeBron wins a gold medal with the U.S. Men's Basketball team at the 2008 Olympic Games.	The Detroit Red Wings win hockey's Stanley Cup.
2010	LeBron becomes the third reigning NBA MVP to change teams.	The New Orleans Saints win their first Super Bowl.

Words to Know

All-Star Game: an annual exhibition basketball game

charity: an organization that collects money for people in need

contract: a signed agreement

draft: the annual selection of players by teams in a professional sports league

endorse: to publicly support a product through advertisements

extreme athletes: people who participate in sporting activities that are dangerous

fouled: broke the rules of the game by making contact with another player

franchise: a professional sports team

professional: someone who is paid for his or her work

rebounds: taking possession of a ball that has bounced off the backboard or rim

rookie: someone new to a field of work

scholarships: financial aid given to a student with good grades or special skills

scouts: people who are employed to observe and report on the strategies and players of sports teams

stability: not subject to sudden or extreme change

tuition: payment for instruction

Index

Log on to www.av2books.com

AV² by Weigl brings you media enhanced books that support active learning. Go to www.av2books.com, and enter the special code found on page 2 of this book. You will gain access to enriched and enhanced content that supplements and complements this book. Content includes video, audio, web links, quizzes, a slide show, and activities.

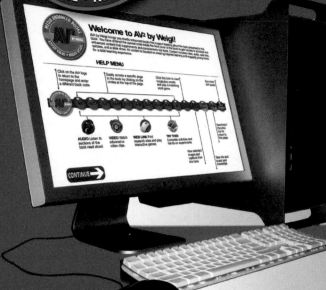

Audio
Listen to sections of the book read aloud.

Video
Watch informative video clips.

Embedded Weblinks
Gain additional information for research.

Try This!
Complete activities and hands-on experiments.

WHAT'S ONLINE?

Try This!	**Embedded Weblinks**	**Video**	**EXTRA FEATURES**
Complete an activity about your childhood.	Learn more about LeBron James' life.	Watch a video about LeBron James.	**Audio** Listen to sections of the book read aloud.
Try this activity about key events.	Learn more about LeBron James' achievements.	Check out another video about LeBron James.	**Key Words** Study vocabulary, and complete a matching word activity.
Complete an activity about overcoming obstacles.	Check out this site about LeBron James.		
Write a biography.			**Slide Show** View images and captions, and prepare a presentation.
Try this timeline activity.			**Quizzes** Test your knowledge.

AV² was built to bridge the gap between print and digital. We encourage you to tell us what you like and what you want to see in the future.

Sign up to be an AV² Ambassador at www.av2books.com/ambassador.